T0065567

Smile . . .
It Becomes
You!!!

Doctor M. E. Lyons

authorHOUSE®

AuthorHouse™
1663 Liberty Drive
Bloomington, IN 47403
www.authorhouse.com
Phone: 1 (800) 839-8640

Published by AuthorHouse 08/25/2016

ISBN: 978-1-5246-2618-1 (sc)
ISBN: 978-1-5246-2617-4 (e)

Print information available on the last page.

This book is printed on acid-free paper.

KJV
Scripture quotations marked KJV are from the Holy Bible, King James
Version (Authorized Version). First published in 1611. Quoted from the KJV
Classic Reference Bible, Copyright © 1983 by The Zondervan Corporation.

Book Dedication

This book is dedicated to every person who struggles with smiling, having a good time, enjoying life and who has been miserable. I believe that smiling is the remedy to many of the issues we struggle with on a daily basis.

Introduction

In almost all of my texts, messages, and emails
I try and leave this five letter remedy for all
who communicate with me: SMILE!

Contents

Chapter One

"Laughter Precept"

⌐Laughter is good for the soul. Proverbs prescribes that a merry heart is like a medicine. In so many words, the more we laugh the healthier we are. Laughter lends life!
M.E. Lyons

"Laugh…Out…Loud…"
Philippians 4:4

BRB-be right back
IDK- I don't know
ROTF-rolling on the floor
TTYL- talk to you later
WYD-what you doing
IKR- I know right
OMG- oh my God
HMU- hit me up
SMH- shaking my head
BFF- best friend forever

Face booking, tweeting, and texting…

Many folks these days are down about
so many things in life…

Tis not only adults down…but elderly people…I just read in the room online that Social Security is being threatened to be cut off completely…just down…

Adults…because there is seemingly no promise in the physical for the future…

Young folk…are dying younger and younger at the hands of other younger folk…

Just plenty that could have heads hung down…

Undeniably so we now live in a day whereas everything is so fast paced…

And with the fast pace in society there has even been an unusual demand to conversate with as less letters as possible…

Satan desires to kill our weapon of warfare and that is our tongue…

Because time has dictated that words occupy too much time; so in response shorthand and acronyms are to now supposed to fit the dictates of our surroundings…

You see because now hurry has suggested that we should rush through everything…

Now what has taken place is joy, happiness, and excitement have been replaced with sadness, silence, and settling…

What we have here in the text is that Paul's
life has now been posted on the original
Facebook homepage of King Nero…

His life now is comfortless, seemingly hopeless, and
even dreary but to our surprise he gives us something
to hold on to…while it seems better to let go of…

When this passage is read properly it connotes
that to rejoice is to laugh and be joyful…

Watch this: Paul did not urge us to be happy because
there are several situations that silence happiness…

But we can draw strength from possessing joy…

Look at Paul he had nothing to be happy
about; but he could find some joy…

If it were not so Paul would not have later
suggested to be careful for nothing…

Listen: Rejoice in Greek means cairo…
to be happy, well off, glad…

But watch this in salutations it means on meeting or
parting, which suggests that when we see a person and
we leave a person…we ought to inspire them to L.O.L.

We are not to do this sometimes but
Paul suggests at all times…

Doctor M. E. Lyons

Although everything else changes; the Lord does not…

Paul says for us to rejoice…

Now he is on death row and says to
us be excited…exuberated…

I mean that is almost like a person that cannot
see saying boy that sun sure is beautiful…

You see how can you interest me to rejoice
when I see crying in your situation…

Why…does Paul not say cry and
again I say cry in the Lord…

OMG…

He then ties our Joy into a specific place…
You see joy can only be found in the LORD…

He even tells us where we can go to
have the joy dispensed…

Beloved to be joyful is to be completely happy…

The Lord is the inexhaustible source of joy…

Then Paul says…in the Lord and literally
means in union with the Lord; which further
implies that we live with him…

Because when two becomes one; they
OUGHT to live with each other...

Then in the Lord...says that when you are with him the
only way to keep joy is to give it to him which suggests
in order to keep the joy you have to get the mess out...

But then he throws another curve
because he says ALWAY...

This word always with no s has bothered me
for years and found out that it means <u>pawn-
tah-tay</u>, which means EVERY WHEN...

Now watch this; every when in our
life is infinite and eternal...

When trouble assails us
When life seems unfair
When problems become many
When sickness comes...
When our BFF upsets us...
When our boy starts tripping...
When IDK...WYD begins to make me SMH...
instead of OMG but it really is L.O.L....

Well, IDK about you but L.O.L. is in order and I
am looking for some folk that can say OMG is so
good you have to restate what He has done...

You see I then researched this business of the colon
being set in the middle of this sentence...

A colon's sole purpose is to tell you what to do, and
then tells you what to do about what to do…

Because watch this…it can introduce a list…. Pastor Lyons
is a radical preacher: because he doesn't mind preaching,
singing, stomping, and shouting at the same time…

But then, it can introduce a restatement
of the previous clause: Rejoice in the Lord
always: and again I say rejoice…

Or it can introduce an elaboration
of the previous statement…

This means that your previous statement is
followed with a more inspirational display…

OMG…

IAFNM-I aint for no mess...

Rejoice in the conclusion says uncontainable…

I dare you to shake a neighbor's hand and tell
them one thing God has done for you…

Then look back at them and say IKR…

You really ain't telling me anything
I do not already know…

TTYL…Holler at your boy…

Next Sunday if the Lord says the same I will BRB…

If the Lord has done anything for you when service
ends; find me on Facebook and HMU…

When you login and begin to tweet and
Facebook tell the world WYD…

I dare you to tell everybody in Facebook world
I have created a new Acronym…GGTP…

Giving God the Praise…

I dare somebody in here tonight to go and find somebody
else and say you know what I am doing I am GGTP-ing…

Since I am
GGTP-ing I can't help but to L.O.L…

Chapter Two

"Struggle Precept"

~Struggles are things that we care not to ever experience.
If it were not for struggles there would be no appreciation
for the successes of life. The Holy Writ declares
that His strength is made perfect in our weakness.
Struggles suggest success is right around the corner!
M.E. Lyons

"When struggle has a baby"
James 1:2-4

It is imperative to hasten to impute and impress upon the
very carriages of your mind that life can seemingly present
itself as unfair...

It would behoove and become us to come to the vast reality
that cataclysmic is the course that many of us have come...

Maybe you have not reached that point; but isn't it somewhat
troubling to get one thing straightened out to discover four
more have surfaced...

I must submit to you this day that James is on target when
he boldly suggests that troubles will assail us...

I almost feel as if James offers as consolation to us that it really does not matter whose family you are in; situations will present themselves…

I hate to upset your pretty presuppositions but James is the brother of Jesus; and he says don't worry trouble is coming…

I mean how can you open a conversation saying hey brother be happy when struggles presents itself!

I don't know about you but I am somewhat confused as to why James begins by saying to us that just because I am a leader does not exempt me from struggles…

I wish I had someone who could understand that just because you are a pastor, deacon, mission sister, or laity we are not exempt from struggling…

I do appreciate how he mentions this struggle though; he says my brethren, as if to say we are in this thing together…

I understand your ministry may be this and mine may be that but we are on the same team…my brethren…

I know my geographical location may differ from yours; but brethren.

I understand your marquee may read different than my marquee but brethren.

I know your way of worship may differ from my way of worship but as long as we meet up in spirit and in truth… my brethren…

Count it all joy...

Now watch how he sucks us into a sad situation but dresses it up with happy clothes...

He says count it joy when trouble comes; struggles arise.

Trials do come to make us strong...

The word trial means to stretch...

To expand…to utilize the elasticity component that resides in us…

Trials can mean from within; or those that are inflicted from without.

But what rattles me is the introductory word to the subject matter is when!

The very mentioning of the word when suggests that it is inevitable, inexcusable, inescapable, and unavoidable and that it will take place…

We just need not miscarry what should be.

Trials.

We must realize we cannot speed up the process…

When

Because patience needs to have her perfect work…

Telios- comb…

When the word perfect is used it is not used as being perfect but rather that the trial will not overtake us.

Otherwise what we are in; we know we will be over.

Divers (diverse) temptations (people and phenomenon) mean various trials…

If I had to paint a picture I would tell you it means that when folk that don't mean you no good …don't worry, you'll have the last laugh…

Situations that had you worried will now have you winning…

Circumstances that made you praying will now have you praising…

Watch this: James says you will have the last laugh…

It's right there in the text he says it in his introduction… brethren count it all joy…

And joy here means to have a good time to laugh.

Doctor M. E. Lyons

We used to say the same thing that'll make you laugh will make you cry…

But James says the same thing that'll make you cry will make you laugh…

Otherwise when you are having trouble; don't start crying as if something has happened…

Start laughing because you know the outcome.

I know it seems hard but if you expected it then it wouldn't hurt so badly.

Come on he says when folk lie on you just go ahead and count it all joy…

Scandalize your name
Run rumors on you
Stab you in the back
Start mess
Hurt your feelings

Then James teaches us about the word count.

Count in this scripture means to command, in Greek it is: Haig-eh-om-ahee.

Which simply means it may be hard…but command yourself to laugh in the face of the enemy.

Force yourself to have joy when it seems all is lost.

We are to rejoice knowing that God is testing us.

Patience is what will make us a full grown Christian.

Evidently some Christians have never really grown up.

Patience comes through suffering and testing.

You'll grow up when God finishes working patience.

Jean Jacques Rousseau

In the mid 1700's said: "patience is bitter,

but its fruit is sweet".

Work in the fourth verse is a derivative of the word labour…

You know what labour means don't you…?

When labour is used here it means periodic contractions.

Don't allow every trial and every struggle having you wanting to throw in the towel.

If I threw in the towel every time I had a little struggle, I would have run out of towels a long time ago.

The baby would not be conceived…Joy…

What I'm saying here is don't allow the struggles of life to turn you around!

Doctor M. E. Lyons

Keep holding on to the Word of God.
Because if you struggle you ought to know the outcome.

Count it all joy…

I believe those are the sentiments that the song was implying
"This joy that I have the world…"

Cigars-all I have are some handshakes…hugs…and high
fives…

Receiving blanket…receive it…

Tell somebody: my life is a little bloody but the baby has
arrived…

One seasoned preacher said: some of our sermons don't have
enough blood on it…

Chapter Three

"Concept Precept"

-When we accept the fact that everything happens for a reason; our concept of the why's in our life would direct us to the when's in our lives. So when we are in the middle of our why's expect the when's to appear directly.
M.E. Lyons

"When God flips the script"
Genesis 50:20

Isn't it strange that the more you try and help a person the more they try and tear you down?

Because this is what is transpiring in the text; you try and assist family and they try to rain on your parade.

I mean I know there are a few more witnesses that have bent over backwards for somebody in your family and then in return for thanks they stabbed you in the back.

Maybe it wasn't a family member, perhaps it was a friend whom you would have given your last dime, and now it's a different story.

I know there may be someone here that says it was somebody in the church house that got me good.

But the Lord has strategically placed me in this place this day to declare that God will flip the script.

Folk want to disappoint your dreams.

This message was built for those who have scars.

Those whom hurt have resided for years.

For those who have been awakened by what others have done to them and will not go away.

God uses what's uncomfortable for me that cause my pain to teach.

God allows weakness to set in, in order for His strength to put on display.

The question I have this morning is what sermon are we preaching from our scars.

What are we preaching from the pulpit of our pain?
God is present in our pain.

The reason we ought to know that He is because look at Joseph;

Sold to Ishmaelites
Put in Potiphars house
Thrown in jail
Cupbearer to the king

It may look bad but this is only the introduction!

But then God has a purpose in my pain!

Otherwise I do not go through what I go through for no reason!

Come here, I need to slow down long enough to share with some person here that where you are in life right now does not take place without a purpose.
(Tell somebody there is a purpose...)

Watch this:
In every place Joseph was placed, he became stronger!

Watch this now, he was sold as a slave, but in ended up being the one over all the slaves.

He was thrown in prison, but ended up being over all the prisoners.

He was the cupbearer and in charge of everything under the king.
Then Joseph was the same one whom the brothers had to come back and beg for food!

Three sakes:
My sake
Other's sake
His sake

David says He leadeth me in the paths of righteousness for His names sake.

Now watch this it takes thirteen chapters to tell Josephs story from being kicked, prodded, picked on and everything else until it was all changed.

Otherwise my deliverance may not come over night but if I keep moving along in my life chapter fifty will come.

But then in chapter 42 they had no food in their homeland of Canaan, and they came to where Joseph was.

Scripture says Joseph acted strange so they wouldn't know who he was.

Now they key here is that although someone has done you wrong you ought not to want revenge, revenge is mines saith the Lord.

I wish you would tell somebody I don't need revenge I just need a flipped script.
But notice his own brothers didn't recognize him.

He asked them for some background history:

They said this is all of us, oh except our youngest brother he is at the house with our daddy.

Joseph said I tell you what your request will be granted upon one condition, go and fetch that brother.

So the second time famine makes it to Canaan Josephs' hometown and his brothers have no grain and have to travel to Egypt to buy some, they just didn't realize who they would be buying from.

He has every right to play the victim.

Now watch how Joseph uncovers his scars: genesis 45:1-8.

He cried out leave, everyone leave.

No one knew these were his brothers, he intended to not endanger them.

But Joseph cried so loudly the Egyptians heard him outside.

They went and told pharaoh.

He said: is my father still alive?

He said come closer to me, in case it was nothing to you.

I am Joseph your brother, the one you sold into Egypt.

He said but don't feel badly…

Otherwise I am glad it happened.

You ought to tell somebody I'm glad that happened to me;

It made me a better man/woman

I'm glad I lost that house...he had a better one for me anyway...

He says don't blame yourself for selling me... God was behind it.

I know you did it, but He used you to do it in order to get me to where I am.

God sent me ahead of you to save lives.

Actually He used you to sell me so that when the famine came I might be able to feed you...

I wish somebody who sho'nuff filled with the Holy Ghost to get up and tell somebody God used you so that I might be able to bless you...

I know you may not have meant good for me but He did!

It wasn't you it was God.

Through scars, pains, rejection, and separation and he is thanking them for what they did.

Joseph teaches us we ought to have 50:20 vision.

Otherwise what we are dealing with ought not to depress us.

Watch this Joseph never used his pain to for payback.

Our problem is, if someone wrongs us we have to get them back.

But notice how much better God is at this than us.

Listen to how God words this blessing in disguise.

He firstly addresses those who are the oppressor he says: but as for you…

Which is to say I'll handle you…?

He says the oppressor ends up being the oppressed in order that God might turn it around.

Watch this; he did not say what they meant for evil as we often say…

He says ye thought…

I'm trying to drive it home for you.

The word thought in Hebrew means:
Weave, fabricate, or imagine…

Now follow me here if I were to imagine I had a million dollars that wouldn't buy me what I wanted.

If someone was to fabricate, it means they lied, so the truth might be in there but is has been twisted somewhere.

Doctor M. E. Lyons

But if I used the original word weave it gives a stronger interpretation.

Otherwise weave is to take something that is not yours and make it appear that it is.

Remember a woman's hair in these days is their glory.

So what he says here is what they cogitated in their mind appears to be in their favor but it actually does not belong to them.

So when I look through 50:20 vision I see that:

Sickness
Crime
Destruction of families
Oppression
Economy
Socialism
Employment

50:20 vision says despite the evidence God is at work.

He takes evil and switches it to and for our good.

In Genesis one: He says it is all good.

But man messes that up by chapter 3.

God uses the slavery of Joseph to save his family.

Brothers meant evil

Potiphar's wife meant evil

Cupbearers neglect

Seven years of famine

But you have to wait long enough for God to bring good

out of evil.

God took what you started wrong and made it end well.

Otherwise the story doesn't end here.

I will not die until god says it's over...

Verse 26.
Even while Paul was in prison he writes for we know that
all things...

He uses the death of Jesus to save the world.

We should never ask for a scar to be removed...

It will remind us of what God brought us through.

Paul says I asked the Lord three times...

Wounds and scars open a 50:20 vision to see a better way.

Abuse

Remember when Jesus came out of the tomb He still had scars...

In the book "The Jesus I never knew" by Phillip Yancey says: Jesus could have picked anybody he desired but he chose the one with the scars.

Scars never really go away!

Satan thought on Good Friday that his evil would win, but that was only the introduction.

The conclusion was on Sunday morning!

Come on go find somebody not sitting close to you and say this is only my introduction, my conclusion will be greater.

Jesus made evil crawl into the crevices of the cross and commit suicide because when He died, evil was turned to good.

Somebody sold Jesus too, and was abused but he was only there to get us "to here.

Chapter Four

"Exchange Precept"

~It has been said that crying is a type of cleansing.
The only thing that needs to be added to this is the
reason why we cry. We cry because of the calling
on our lives to birth the convictions in our lives.
M.E. Lyons

"Don't get upset its setup"
Psalms 30:5

(Expound- Think of difficult times)

Somebody on your job
Sisters & their husbands
Husbands
Children
Pastors

*Anthropomorphic- the hand of the Lord

• verse 1 the resolve- lifted me up-delivered them

The reasons- thou hast not made mine enemies rejoice
over me.

(You ought to have something to shout about)

Doctor M. E. Lyons

Verse 5 Endureth- continuous

endureth but- italicized- can be replaced
you could be broke, but
you could be sick, but
you could be lonely, but
you can be w/out a husband, but
bills are due, but

moment- how long is a moment
come here let me tell you- I don't know but I know it's
shorter than a lifetime.

In his favour is- italicized he can be that for you

Your doctor
Lawyer
Midnight rider
Sister
Brother
Money
Company-keeper

But it goes on to say

Is- life, so he can be these things but it's for life.

You ever knew anybody to do something for you but only
for that one time.

Life is designed for us to experience evening before morning.

It's designed for us to see darkness before light, even in the morning its dark before its light

Sorrow is associated w/ night & songs for daylight, but a saint can sing a song in during the night hours.

It's not how long your nights are; the question is how long you make your nights.

The psalmist makes statement weeping may- it can last for a night, but the one sure thing is that joy is coming.

When it comes it's all up to you.

It's when you figure out that you been set up by God to be blessed that you can be blessed.

That job you lost- it's a setup
That friend that betrayed you- it's a setup
That spouse that left you- it's setup
That bank account that's at a negative- its setup
Those bills that you can't pay- it's a setup

Are you upset?

Daniel in the Lion's den
Joseph & his brothers
Three Hebrew boys
Paul & Silas
Job

When you realize that you've been setup

Doctor M. E. Lyons

You can receive that what you need

When you realize that you've been set-up

You can receive that all things work together blessing.

When you realize that you've been setup to be blessed

You'll get that pressed down, shaken together & running over blessing.

When you realize that you been set up

You can see God on a sunny day, opening up the windows of heaven & pouring the blessings that you don't have room enough to receive.

Chapter Five

"Command Precept"

"It's Coming Together
Ezekiel 37

~The Bible teaches us to ask and it shall be given.
The precept of commanding things to take place
is a very real principle that we must practice. We
learn to command in our communication during
our conflict we can expect a coming out party!

*"What we say spiritually will be what we see;
and what we see is a direct result of what we sow!"*

M.E. Lyons

William James said: "We are like islands in the sea,
separate on the surface, but connected in the deep!"

Bones represent death.

Bones represent the lack of.

Bones signify that there is some
disconnectedness somewhere.

Bones also represent structure

Bones also serve as an outline of what the
finished product should be shaped.

But notice the line of questioning:
God asks: "What do you see?"

Ezekiel saw bones; but God saw an army!

You see a struggling black man;
God sees a business owner.

You see a broken family; God sees a
testimony ready to share.

You see sickness; God sees an opportunity for a miracle.

You're looking at what is; He is looking at what shall be!

Point: We need the SPIRIT to handle our SITUATIONS.

The spirit of the Lord CARRIED him out
IN the VALLEY of dry BONES.

You see the spirit makes the difference.

The spirit is the determining factor
between life and death.

No spirit; death; have the spirit there is life.

For the Holy Writ ascribes that where the
spirit of the Lord is there is liberty!

Carried means to go <u>FORWARD</u>.

Toward something
With a purpose
Deliverance
In a certain direction

Notice that he carried him around to
<u>LOOK</u> at what was the issue.

He wanted him to see how bad things were in order to
appreciate how much better they were going to be!

<u>LOOK</u> at your situation and wait on the wind!

<u>LOOK</u> at how much hell has been in
your home; now wait on the wind.

<u>LOOK</u> at how many things have gone
wrong; now wait on the wind.

<u>LOOK</u> at how awful folk have treated
you; now wait on the wind!

BUT, then the word behold also means <u>POKER</u>!

Now the Holy Spirit is not only represented
by wind but it represents FIRE!

When I was younger and it would get chilly; they would
start a fire in the fire place and they had what was called
a stoker which in the country we called it a <u>POKER</u>.

The <u>POKER's</u> purpose was to poke the log to keep the fire going and even increase the flames purpose.

So when God took Ezekiel on the tour he <u>POKED</u> the situation in order to get more out of the log than what he could see!

<u>Point: We Will then have power to SPEAK to our STRONGHOLDS.</u>

Prophesy means to be under the influence!

We cannot legitimately prophesy without being under the influence.
(Talk about how alcohol renders an under the influence feeling.)

<u>Point: OBEDIENCE gives birth to ORDER.</u>

The enemy is after our STRUCTURE!

Beloved, when Ezekiel did what God had ordered him to do things began to come together and fall in order.

The bones being disconnected proved that things were OUT OF ORDER!
Families were OUT OF ORDER.
Marriages were OUT OF ORDER.
Friendships were OUT OF ORDER.
Minds were OUT OF ORDER.

When we begin to move in obedience
things will begin to come together.

Let me tell you what this entire Sermon
is about: SOMETHING HAPPENS
WHEN WE COME TOGETHER!

Yes, we can do things by ourselves; but
we are better when we have

Because when we connect things happen.

When we connect: we go from being
BONES to being an ARMY!

An army is only brought together to do one thing!

An army is assembled to win a war!

I am declaring war FOR MY FAMILY
I am declaring war FOR MY FUTURE
I am declaring war FOR MY FINANCES

Chapter Six

"Environment Precept"

˷Stop letting your environment intrude on the inside of your life; the problem is not being in the environment it is when you allow the environment to get on the inside of you; Consider the ship/vessel it traverses on water, in water, through water and water is the environment but the issue can only be discouraging when what is the environment of the ship now invades the ship/vessel; then the ship/vessel begins to take on the water and becomes overwhelmed by that which was the source of carrying it from point a to point b.

M.E. Lyons

"What Do You See?"
Mark 8:24

This is only recorded in the synoptic Gospel of Mark.

Louie Armstrong has a song:
"What A Wonderful World."

I see trees of green, red roses, too,
I see them bloom, for me and you
And I think to myself
What a wonderful world.

The world to any one person is only as
beautiful as how they see it.

Deal with how a person perceives a thing.

One person may complain and fuss while
another sees a thing entirely different.

The problem is that we have an obtrusive optical outlook.
We should possess an open and optimistic outlook.

Stop entertaining your exterior and allow it to be
an excuse to interrupt the intent of your interior.

The blind man saw what his mind had
pre-conditioned itself to see.

He saw trees while others saw men; this is
not only literal but it is also figurative.

The issue with so many is that their optics are
obstructed by that which has served as an obstacle.

Obstacles are only outlets to promote opportunities.

Jesus took him by the hand and he could
have taken him to his friends but he decided
to take him to his destiny himself.

Out of the city; denotes that those who were
in the city were not qualified to take part.

Doctor M. E. Lyons

Sometimes it pays to <u>NOT</u> be in the in-crowd.

Bethsaida is known for being a place of fish
and the word Bethsaida itself means: fishing
house. How can you be known as a fishing
house but no fish are caught in the house?

Allow me to make it tad bit clearer: It is
like saying I can see but you miss me!

One music blind composer said there is
nothing worse than being blind other than
having sight and still cannot see.

That is what these people were guilty of: their
optical tests yielded 20/20 vision but their potential
progress was yielding them spiritually blind.

Perhaps the reason he took him out of the city is because
they would not be able to <u>SEE WHAT THEY SAW!</u>

Because some people only see what they
have perceived in their mind.

If the glass is half empty that is all that it will ever be.

You see we must be critically carefully to not see what our
mind desires over and against what the obvious offers.

The mind will receive that no one in your
family has ever went to college; but the
obvious is that you can break the cycle.

The mind will receive that there is a set standard and mold to stay within; while the obvious suggests that there are no rules of engagement in progress.

Your mind will receive that everyone who desires to make it thinks outside the box; while the obvious suggests that the best way is to burn the box and possess <u>NO BOX THINKING</u>!

You see our mind will receive that blindness is the inevitable; while the obvious offers Jesus is in front of you.

Now if Jesus is in front of you; there are no restrictions, constrictions or chains.

Why was the initial healing not fully restoration?

He was seeking to see if partially he could understand so that when the full reveal is made that he would be able to perceive it.

Now Jesus did this broken down into two treatments.

Understand that in verse 21 Jesus asks a rhetorical question: how can you not understand after I've had fed the four thousand?

If I fed four thousand on a <u>FRAGMENT</u>; I can do much with your <u>BROKEN</u> lives.

He literally says to them: you have eyes but you cannot see!

In other words, you must be form Bethsaida.

The disciples were blind as well.

Jesus does something very unusual
and spits on the man's eyes.

Watch this, people of this day believed that
spittle and saliva had healing power and Jesu
cared enough to honor what he believed.

What do you do when you burn or cut your
finger; you stick it in your mouth?

The saliva seems to ease the pain.

Jesus started where the man was with saliva and took
him to where he needed to be with his touch.

Then he asks the man a question: "What Do You See?"

He then looked up and said: I see men as trees.

He must had seen before in life because he said
I see men as trees; how else would he know?

He then touched his eyes and made him look up.

The answer to your problem maybe where you are looking
because usually those who are blind and expect nothing
see nothing because originally the man was looking down.

What Do You See? I see men as trees walking; Jesus TOUCHED his eyes and then MADE the man LOOK UP.

After two elevations you have not only left seeing the ground, but you now have left seeing what's ahead and now you focus on the Heavens.

Now; What Do You See? The scripture says; he could see clearly now that the rain is gone!

He told him to go home; but to not go in town.

Could it be that he was teaching him that the reason you could not see to start out with was because of your environment.

People see what is around them and it hinders what he could possibly see.

He did tell the man to go home. There was something about home.

He was a burden to his home at first but now he can be a blessing.

The Christmas hymn says: do you see what I see; no I see what is intended for me to see.

Chapter Seven

"Woo-Saa Precept"

~Somethings in life are meant for us to give up instead
of hold onto. Consider Jacob and the angel in the
book of Genesis. Jacob was holding on to so many
things that God wanted him to let go of and it was
not until he let go that he had a new lease on life.
M.E. Lyons

"Let it go…"
Hebrews 12: 14, 15

Isn't it strange how what we used to say stick and stones
may hurt my bones but words can never hurt me…?

This has been and is a grand ole' lie…because
words can hurt…so much that the words that we
hear can be held onto for years after our bones
have healed from the sticks and stones…

You know how it is for to have had someone hurt
you so deeply it took days, weeks, and perhaps
even years to be able to muster a smile…

I need to grasp the attention of that person who
can have a great day and all of the sudden someone

who has hurt you walks in the room and that great
day has now turned into your worse day...

I want to speak into the life of that married couple
who struggle to stay together based on the mistakes
your previous spouse or mate put you through...

To that individual that had who they thought
was their friend stab them in the back...

That person who came to church to find a sweet
resolution only to experience someone at Church
mistreat you worse than those on the outside...

I stand this day to hope some person here
to see the necessity in letting it go...

Listen very attentively to what Paul suggests
to us about this silent killer...

You see holding on is much easier than letting it go...

That's why he says: Looking diligently...otherwise
BEWARE...and when he says beware he literally implies
WATCH OUT because this will eat you away...

Strongholds...a false pattern of thinking...

A bitter person becomes a prisoner of his own
making; he is angry, discord- aged depression.

How can we tear down strongholds?

If we have given ground to satan…

We are under his influence…

You have been mean to me and saying nothing
was wrong but you won't let it go…

Throw it down…give it up…let it go…

Now don't take it out on me because you are mad at
what your last boyfriend/girlfriend did to you…

I cannot stand you…but the sad indictment is: you
are not affecting me you are affecting yourself…

You see when bitterness begins to set in: you will
be walking away and somebody says something
and you will say: what did they say about me?

I mean you hold onto everything: can you remember
Tuesday on the 13th of July while we were in T.G.I.
Fridays and you were eating the Chicken and cheese
dinner with a coke and you said such and such…

What we have done is redefined what bitterness is: and
we will say I'm not bitter…I am just deeply hurt…

So now you have it tucked away in your
file cabinet of your mind…

What you have constituted as hurt has festered ad become
bitterness…and nobody can do right concerning you…

Smile . . . It Becomes You!!!

She ain't right
He sure ain't right
I don't like my job
They get on my nerves
The choir can't sing
I can't stand the Pastor

It's too sunny
It's too chilly
Food ain't right
Water is nasty

You begin to get angry with everybody
and everything…just release it…

You see darkness is satan's playground…so the person that
is bitter is living in darkness and is under satan's power…

You better get a grip on your bitterness…

Springing means to puff up or to swell…you will
be walking around thinking you are the one who is
right; only to find out you are the one troubled…

Everything rests in the closet of our minds…

The word trouble in the text means to crowd…

Bitterness will crowd your mind and emotions
so; that there is no room for anything else…love
forgiveness, peace of mind, joy, concern…etc.

You see because when you are bitter; it shows…someone
can just show up and now you are mad all over again…

You better let it go before you lose your business
Your friends walk away
Your break up your family
Your marriage is tore up
Your position is done away with
You get fired

You lose everything you have looking backwards…

Has someone ever said something or done something
to you that you could not forgive them…

Every time their very name came up…butterflies begin
to flap their wings in the center of your tummy…

You cannot stand the sight of them…
When you think of them your heart begins to
palpitate…so now, you are a prisoner of bitterness…

Your blood pressure rises…you are now
reliving it all over again…

The other person continues to live
while you are worrying…

They ain't even studying you and you
taking pills trying to sleep at night…

They control your life…

Now you are calling people names…
We cannot control what happens in life but
we can control how we respond…

Look into marriages these days…you are hurt
and fifteen years later just sitting at the house
and nobody is saying anything to anybody…

Riding around town and the car ride is silent…

If you can't give a word give a wink…

Whereas you used to be; Lovey dovey…
huggy huggy…kissy kissy…

Bitterness has stripped everything you used to have…

Now you start calling people by names of
folk you were hurt and can't stand…

Be quiet with your Myron looking self…

You act just like your daddy/mama…

You hear somebody say this is the day that
the Lord…and you roll your eyes…

What you are doing is holding back from
them all that they deserve…love

Bitterness will destroy you physical…
it enters your subconscious mind…

It runs while you are sleeping…angry
in your sleep…. wake up mad…

Medical doctors say bitterness will
affect your body…and health…

It can cause: glandular issues…high blood pressure…
cardiac disorders…. ulcers, and even sanity…

Then you are on a look what id didn't do tandem…

Drove all the gas out of the car…I didn't
cook…I said my head was hurting…

But while you are holding out you are being eaten away…

I ain't fixing anything around the house….

When it comes to Church you will say I
ain't gone work nor do anything…

I ain't gone say amen…I ain't going to do
anything the Pastor asks me to do…

But it's you that spend your time trying to figure
out how to make somebody else's life a living
hell when it's really your life that is hell…

Examine what God calls those who do these
things…verse 8…if I tell you and you still don't do
it you are bastards and do not belong to me…

Smile . . . It Becomes You!!!

Some folk have become as hateful as a burnt cat...

Bitterness leads to paranoia...

You will start to develop a victim's mentality...
tweedy bird...I tought I taw a pussy cat...

Ain't nobody after you...

Lick your wounds and get over it...

Grow up...

God allows us to be hurt sometimes to

see if we will be bitter or better...

Bitterness divides fellowship...you don't know
what happened...it doesn't matter...

Bitterness divides relationships...
there is a spillover effect...

You don't have to be bitter toward your
spouse to mess up your marriage...

You can be bitter with somebody at
Church and ruin your marriage...

You can bitter with an old friend and the new friend
feels the effect...what's wrong with you today...

Nothing...well something is...spillover effect...

They could even be dead and you are still bitter…they
could owe ten dollars and you are spending thousands
of dollars on medicine for a ten-dollar debt…

It will deprive you of a blessing…
because it follows you to Church…

You will not come to Church looking for a blessing you
will come to see what's wrong…and you will find it…

You will come to see who the Pastor
is preaching about now…

Coming to see what is the latest tea…

How can we remove the root of bitterness…?

Yank it up by the root…

Children of Israel crossed Red Sea…they
were thirsty but came to Marrah…

How did God tell Moses to fix it?

Cut down the tree…yank up the roots… touch
that which is bitter…the waters were healed…

You have to pull it up…it may be messy
but bitterness can be made sweet…

Because every day with Jesus is sweeter…

Then the word defile means to contaminate…

You see contaminate means: to be harmful and unusable…

If a river is where we get our water has been
used as a dumping place the trash has made
the water that was good unusable…

When God created us we were good…but when trash
is continuously dumped in us we become unusable…

I refuse to keep letting twenty years ago…

Five years ago
Last week
Yesterday

Keep me from my blessing…

The question is: Do you have power to
love those who hated on you…

Done you wrong
Lied on you
Broke your heart
Mishandled your commitment
Trampled on your love
Abandoned you
Abused you
Harmed your family in some way
Broke up your marriage
Fractured your friendship

Because God said overcome evil with good…

Let it go…go find three folks and say let it go…

Let go of the anger
Let go of the malice
Let go of the hate
Let go of the division
Let go of the depression
Let go of the bitterness
Let go of the grudge
Let go of the I'mma get'em back mentality

LET IT GO…

Really…what we need is true restoration…when something is messed up really bad…restoration is in order…

Psalms 23:3 he restoreth my soul…

Printed in the United States
By Bookmasters